Use
IPHONE
8/8 Plus

Like A Crazy Expert

Updated iPhone 8 manual for
beginners and seniors

Stephen W. Rock

Dedicated to all my readers

Acknowledgement

Ii want to say a very big thank you to Michael Lime, a 3D builder, my colleague. He gave me moral support throughout the process of writing this book.

Table of Contents

Introduction

The title of this book already gives a hint on what the book is about. It is a guide for new users of the iPhone 8/8 plus.

Dividing the whole book into three parts, the first part introduces you on how to get started with the iPhone 8/8 pus, the middle exposes a comprehensive list of tricks for exploring music, videos, FaceTime etc. The last part culminates with useful camera tricks.

Also, with the comprehensive list of commands, you'll definitely learn to be a pro in using Siri, Apple's voice assistant. You'll be a pro in using Apple Pay. You'll be an iOS 12 pro. Yes, an iOS 12 pro.

Now, start savoring the content of this book.

Chapter One

Touring around the iPhone 8 Plus

NOTES:

Sleep and wake

You might have noticed that after a few minutes, your iPhone just goes off by itself. This can happen automatically or you might even do it by yourself manually with the sleep and wake button. Of course you don't want your iPhone 8 to be awake permanently. You can if you want to.

But you should know that if the device doesn't go to sleep mode, it will exhaust the battery quickly. You want to make sure that your iPhone is locked or in sleep mode. When it comes to altering the consciousness of your phone, there are a few things that you want to know

- **Wake mode.** When it is said that the phone in in wake mode or it is awake, it means that the phone is showing something on the screen. It could be the lock screen, the home screen.

- **Sleep mode.** When it is said that your phone is in sleep mode or asleep, it means that the screen of the phone is dark. The phone being dark doesn't mean that it is off, you can still get calls and notifications
- **Locked.** When it is said that your phone is locked, it means that your phone is awake but you can access the home screen of the phone. You will just be shown the lock screen. This lock screen is the screen that shows up when you wake your device from sleep mode. You can only access notifications, camera, control center and other things from here. If you have any passwords set, it's at this point that you'll have to enter them to access your phone
- **Unlocked.** When your phone is unlocked, that means that there are no restrictions. You are able to access the home screen and all the features of the phone.

To adjust the time that your phone goes to sleep mode automatically

1. Fire up the **Settings** app
2. Choose **Display & Brightness**
3. Choose the **Auto-lock option**
4. From the page, you'll be able to set the time you want before your phone enters sleep mode.

The lock screen

Depending on how you set it, you can have a lot of features accessible from the lock screen. If you would like to access the features that you make use of most times, you can just edit the lock screen of the iPhone 8 and 8Plus to show those features on the lock screen.

You can enable Siri and you can even make the option to reply to messages available. But you should know that the more you make available on the lock screen, the more strangers will be able to access the features on your phone. Since they wouldn't have to type in any passcode or PIN before they can get to the lock screen, the features that you make available will be available for everyone.

1. Go to the **Settings**
2. Select **Touch ID & Passcode**

3. Put in your passcode

4. Move downwards to the **Allow Access when locked**

5. Now you can turn on the options that you would like to be available on the lock screen

If you would like to make your favorite features accessible easily, you can just toggle them on from here. But if you're concerned about privacy and you would want little to be available from the lock screen, just turn of the toggle for the options

Some of the features that you can enable from this place are Today View, control center reply with message, USB accessories, Notification center, Return missed calls and others.

Switching off and on the iPhone 8

If you would like to put the iPhone 8 device to sleep, you can just easily use the side button and the phone will be in sleep mode. This is the way to put the device to sleep manually apart from the automatic lock that happens according to the time you set. You will also use this button to wake the phone

But that's not the only use of the side button, you can also use the button to put the phone off and on. To turn off your phone

1. Press and hold the side button. Do not release. At least not yet

2. When the slider to put off the device, shows up, you can release. To put off the phone, drag the slider.

If you want to turn on the phone, all you have to do is Long press the side button that you used to put it off. After a while, you should see it phone start up by showing the Apple logo.

Inserting a SIM card on your iPhone

When you get your iPhone 8, one of the first things that you would want to do is put a SIM card. So whether you are just trying to get a SIM card in your new iPhone 8 or you want to remove the old SIM card and replace it with another, here is how you'll go about it.

1. The first thing that you want to do in the insetting SIM card process is putting the device off. If you don't power off the iPhone, you risk endangering both the device and the SIM card
   - To turn off your device, press and hold down the Power button and then slide the screen to power off the device.
2. Cut your SIM card to size. As phones get bigger, SIM cards get smaller. Make sure

that your SIM card is the right size. The right size for your iPhone is a Nano SIM

3. Now you want to find yourself a SIM eject tool. I'm pretty sure that you don't have that. In replacement, you just use a paperclip. Paperclip is the best replacement for the SIM eject tool but you can also use a pin or needle.

4. Now you want to locate the SIM card slot on your iPhone. In your iPhone 8, the slot should be at the right side of the device.

5. You should also find a tiny hole just beside the slot. Fix the SIM eject tool in the hole and push. You don't need too much force to do this just a little force and the tray should come out.

6. You don't want to damage the SIM tray so you want to take it out ever so gently.

7. Place the SIM card in the tray with the gold contacts facing down.

8. Fix the SIM card tray back in the phone correctly. Before moving on to the next step, you want to make sure that you inserted the tray all the way in and it's fitted correctly.

9. Press and hold the power button for you to turn on the device. The Apple logo should show and you will be able to use the SIM card.

3D touch

The 3D touch feature was first released with the iPhone 6s. Ever since then the 3D touch has stopped featuring in iPhones. 3D touch is just a technology that is based on the force touch. If force touch sounds familiar to you it's because you've used the feature before.

The 3D touch was available of the Apple Watch and the MacBook. But it wasn't called 3D touch back then it was called Force touch. The feature is just dependent on the amount of force you use to touch the screen. One upgrade from the force touch in the MacBook and the Apple Watch is that this 3D touch features 3 degrees of pressure.

On phones, we all know the normal ways that we use to interact with the screen. We usually use the Tap, Pinch and Swipe gestures to interact with the screen. But with the 3D touch, users get two new features, the Peek and the Pop.

What Peek and Pop means is just the way you use to tap the screen. If you want to perfrom a Peek gesture, you have to just use medium pressure to press the screen. If you press a little harder on the screen, you'll be doing the Pop gesture.

Why the Peek option is beneficial is because, you'll be able to see information about the content that you want to open without actually tapping it to open. Then with the Pop, you can now open up the content that you previewed.

Like for example if you're in the mail app, you don't always have to tap to open up an email for you to read it. You can just take advantage of the Peek and Pop. You can push with medium force to perfrom the Peek and you'll see the preview of the email and if you would like to open it, you can just press harder to do the Pop and open up the message.

Actually this feature is enabled by default on the iPhone 8 and the iPhone 8 Plus but you can also get busy and do some Settings yourself. To access the setting for the 3D touch,

1. Open up the **Settings**
2. Go to **General**
3. Select **Accessibility**
4. Choose **3d Touch.**

When you tap the option for 3D touch, you'll be able to play with the sensitivity and also try out the 3D touch test with the image that is provided

Touch ID

The Touch ID feature on the iPhone 8 and the iPhone 8 Plus is a good measure of security. It saves the fingerprint that you register and it will makes your phone secure with it. So unless someone with the same fingerprint as you unlocks your phone (which can never be possible), your phone and safe.

To set up the Touch ID on the iPhone 8 and the iPhone 8 Plus

1. Enter the **Settings**
2. Select the option for **Touch ID & Passcode**
3. If you have set a passcode or a PIN on your device, you will need to input it for you to continue with the setup
4. If you don't have a passcode set up, you will need to create one. Reason's because Touch ID needs some form of secondary authentication method suppose the Touch

ID option fails. Select the **Turn passcode on** option

5. To add a fingerprint for the Touch ID, choose **Add a Fingerprint**

6. Now you want your finger is dry and clean. Now place it on the home button. Don't press the button, just place it on it. Many like to register with the thumbs. This is because it's the finger that touches the home button the most

7. You have to put your finger on the button again. Follow the instructions given on the screen during setup.

8. You can also add other fingers in the Touch ID setup. You can add the finger of a trusted person.

9. Now you want to turn on the toggle for Apple Pay, iPhone Unlock, iTunes, App Store and Password Auto fill

Setting passcodes on the iPhone 8

You can secure your phone with the Touch ID and make sure that no one else accesses your information. While the Touch ID is a good option, you can consider setting only passcodes. The option for Touch ID is relatively new in the world of smartphone, but when we talk of passcodes, they been around since eternity.

With passcodes, all the confidential, private, personal and sensitive information that you wouldn't like people to see will still be safe. As long as they don't know the codes, they are not going in. Which is a good way to prevent just about anyone from accessing phone.

While you were setting up your iPhone 8 or iPhone 8 Plus, among the options presented to you to set up is a menu asking you to set passcodes. But if you didn't set it like most people, you can still do some digging in the Settings and set it up.

If you would like to set a passcode on your device
1. Go to the **Settings**
2. Choose the option for **Touch ID & Passcode**
3. Select **Turn Passcode On**
4. You can tap **Passcode Options** for you to see other option to set your passcode
5. Put in the passcode

Chapter Two

Lock Screen and Notification

NOTES:

Reach features from the lock screen

The lock screen on the iPhone 8 is not some blank wall. You get some features like the date and the time. In fact, depending on how you customize it, you will be able to view notifications right from the lock screen.

Typing out the long passcode can be tiring so getting features available on the lock screen is a good option. From the lock screen, you can get to open the camera.

If you would like to get to the camera from the lock screen quickly, you can just swipe left. That's not all you can access from the lock screen, you also get to view the control center. All you have to do is to swipe from the bottom.

How to disable notifications on the lock screen

As we just talked about, you can get the notifications to show up in the lock screen. This is a very useful way to get an idea of the messages you receive. When you hear your phone chime, just take a look at the screen and you'll get to know what the notification is talking about.

But while this is easy and convenient, it's also not good when it comes to security. If the notification you get should be private and confidential, the whole world can know what it is by just looking at your phone.

Thankfully you can turn this off if you don't like it

1. Fire up the **Settings**
2. Go to **Notifications**
3. Pick the notification

4. Switch off the option for **Show On Lock Screen**

Do Not Disturb

The Do Not Disturb feature is that feature that you just have to use when you're in your car. Something that you definitely don't want to happen is using your phone when you should be concentrating on the road. That will lead to a high risk of accidents.

When you turn on Do Not Disturb, you don't get distracted. Sometimes we decide not to use our phones when we are in the car, but then we get an urgent notification and we can't keep away. But with Do Not Disturb, you don't get tempted to pick your phone because you don't hear it.

If you would like to use this Do Not Disturb feature

1. Move to the **Settings** app
2. Select **Do Not Disturb**

3. Among the options shown on the page, choose between, **Manually, Automatically** or **When Connected To Car Bluetooth.**

Chapter Three

Typing, Editing and Searching

NOTES

Look Up dictionary

If you've been using older versions of iPhone, you're probably familiar with the feature called Define. That was for the older iPhones, now with the newer iPhone 8 and 8 Plus what you get is the Look Up. From iOS 10, the Define got replaces with the Look Up.

With this you are able to 'Look Up' the definitions of words that you don't know the meaning of. To do this,

1. Long press the word that you would like to know the meaning of
2. Touch the option for **Look Up**
3. Touch the preview given to see a full view

On your iPhone 8, you should have the default Apple dictionary. But you may want to use other definitions from types of dictionaries.

1. Open up the **Settings** app

2. Go to **General**

3. Choose **Dictionary**

4. Select the dictionary that you would want to include

If there's a dictionary that you don't want definitions to be taken from again, you can just delete it. If you would like to delete a dictionary from your iPhone

1. Go to the **Settings** app

2. Touch **General**

3. Choose **Dictionary**

4. Among the dictionary listed, tap the one that you would like to see gone. A check mark to show up

5. Use the back option to back to the menu.

Using the search

You have the search option on your iPhone 8. With this option, you'll be able to search for contents on your iPhone easily. If you want to search for items, using the search will offer it to you and also give you suggestions as you type each word.

If you would like to use this search of option

1. Swipe down from the center of your screen when you're home screen.
2. Tap the search field
3. Type in the word that you want to search.
4. You can get more result on the word by hitting the show more option.

You also get the option for you to edit the Settings of the search.

1. Go to the **Settings**
2. Choose **Siri & Search**

3. Select the apps that you want to edit

How to cut, copy and paste

Typing out texts on the screen can be tiring. It is a lot better if you're trying to type a short amount of text. If you want to type out a whole document, it can be a lot of stress. Instead of retyping the same long thing in another place, you can just use the copy and paste option to copy it from the main page and then paste it in the place you want it to be in.

If you want to use the copy and paste feature you have to long tap the text. If you would like to copy more text, don't worry you can still do that later for now just press and hold one text. After you've long pressed, for you to know that the screen responded to your command, 2 text handles should show up.

Now is the time to select other texts on the page. Just drag one of the handles on the side of the text to the end of the texts that you want to copy. By dragging either handles, you'll be able to copy the whole document. When you've selected all you want to select, an option should appear.

This is the option for you to copy, paste or cut if you want to take the text away from the page and paste in another area. For you to paste a text or texts that you copied or cut, long press on the space you want to paste it in and choose the Paste option.

Chapter Four

Phone Calls and FaceTime

NOTES

Importing contacts

It's no longer a new thing for people to use Gmail or other services to manage their contacts. But when you start your iPhone, you may want to import it to your device. There are many reasons why you would want to transfer your contacts to your iPhone

If you want to import your Google contacts and you've not registered your account on your iPhone,

1. Launch the **Settings**
2. Choose **Passwords & Accounts**
3. Then choose **Add Account**
4. Depending on the account you want to setup to your iPhone, tap it. if you're using Google. Tap the Google logo
5. Enter the email, password and hit **Next**

6. You'll see the option for manage your contacts on the list presented next. Tap **Accept**

7. You now want to choose the options that you want to be available on your iPhone. Choose contacts and then **Save**.

If you've already registered a Google account on your device, you don't have to go through with the process of setting up anything, just

1. Enter the **Settings**
2. Choose **Passwords & Account**
3. Choose your account
4. Turn on contact.

With this, your contacts will be brought to your iPhone from your account. You should be able to view them in the phone app and the contacts.

How to enable call forwarding

Call forwarding is a very useful feature that allows you not to miss any call. By so doing, your iPhone will kind of send the call to another device. This can be a landline. So if you left your device at home, you can just use the call forwarding option to receive a call from another device.

Before you can use this, you want to first set up

1. Launch the **Settings**
2. Select the **Phone** option
3. You should see **Call Forwarding** in the **Calls** area
4. Turn on the switch for **Call Forwarding**
5. Now you want to enter in the numbers that will be used for the call forwarding.

Using call waiting

Call waiting is one feature that you want to enable on your iPhone 8. This is because it allows users not to stop their recent phone call and still answer an incoming phone call. What this means is that if you're calling someone and you get another phone call, you can still answer it without stopping the ongoing call.

If you think this feature is cool and you would like to enable it

1. Slide into the **Settings**
2. Choose the **Phone** option
3. Select **Call Waiting**
4. Turn on the **Call Waiting** to activate it.

Caller ID

When you have Caller ID enabled on your iPhone, you would have your number shown on the screen of the receiver's phone. As you would know, this Caller ID is also Caller Identification. And just as it means, it allows the people that you call to recognize it's you who's calling

You can disable this option if you would not want people to know it's you calling

1. Go to the **Settings**
2. Choose the **Phone**
3. Turn of the toggle for **Show My Caller ID**. If you would like to enable this feature when it's turned off, you can just toggle it on instead

With this anybody that you call will not see your number. Instead of seeing your number on the display, what they'll see is **Restricted** of **Private**.

You should note that if your carrier does not allow this option, you will not be able to change the settings of your Caller ID. You might want to contact your carrier in that case.

Custom ringtones

Something wonderful about the iPhone 8 is that is allows you to be able to change things. You are able to customize and tweak settings to the way you see fit. One prime example is ringtones. You have the ability to dish out ringtones to each contact.

Apart from the reason of wanting to personalize your phone, this option is also beneficial as is it allows you to find out who is calling you without taking a look at the screen. When you hear the ringtone, you can then decide if you want to pick the call or not.

If you want to set this feature
1. Go to the **Phone** app
2. Choose **Contacts**
3. Tap the contact that you want to designate a tone to

4. Choose **Ringtone**

5. Pick the tone that you want to assign

FaceTime audio and video calls

When you use the iPhone 8 and the Plus, your number will be registered to FaceTime. But something that you also want to do is connect your Apple ID to your FaceTime

1. Go to **Settings**
2. Choose **FaceTime**
3. Use your own Apple ID to connect to FaceTime
4. Sign in with your Apple ID

If you would like to make a call with face time

1. Launch the **FaceTime** app
2. Type the name of the person that you want to call in the search bar at the top
3. Choose contact
4. Use the phone button to make an audio call and the video button to make a FaceTime video call

Group FaceTime

As with group FaceTime, you have the opportunity of adding up to 31 people to the group. If you would like to make a group FaceTime call

1. Open the **FaceTime** app
2. Tap the + button that's at the upper corner
3. Put in the number of the user that you want to call with FaceTime
4. You can add the names of the other users to join the group.

Chapter Five

Siri Voice Commands

NOTES

Using Siri

If you've been using previous iPhone devices, then Siri should not be new to you. But for those who just joined the Apple crew recently, you might have been seeing Siri on your device and have no idea what it is. Or you've been hearing your friends talk about it and you are wondering how you can access it on your device.

Well Siri is an assistant. You know how a boss tells his assistant to send messages or call someone for him, that's how Siri is. It works like an assistant except for the part where, she is virtually operated. But in any case you can get Siri to do a lot of things for you.

You can get it to check the weather, get the latest news or to even call someone. But one of the reasons why you may not have discovered Siri is because you don't find an app titled Siri. So with no app for Siri, how then do we access Siri.

With the home button:

If you want to get to Siri on your iPhone 8 and 8 Plus, you can use the home button. Press and hold the button until you hear a sound to tell you that Siri is now available. Now that Siri has been summoned, you can tell it commands or make requests to it. If you have question that you would like to get an answer to, you can just ask Siri and you'll get an answer.

You might be wondering, what can you say to Siri to get it to do stuff?. Not too worry, well cover that in a bit. But if you're done with giving Siri commands, you don't need to press anything to let Siri know that you're done. It will automatically recognize that and go to work. But you can still use the microphone button to let it know you're done.

When using Bluetooth headsets:

If you're using a Bluetooth headset and then it crosses your mind to summon Siri and give it a command, you don't really need to grab your phone and start long pressing the home button. If you have some kind of remote for your Bluetooth device, you're good to go.

All you have to is to just press down on the button at the center and then you should hear a sound to make you to know that Siri is awake for you, and then you make a request. You should know that this button can be the same button that you would use to answer a call. For those who use AirPods, you can still make use of the button at the outside to perform this feature.

How to use hey Siri

So far you know how to summon Siri when you're using your headsets or through the home button on your phone. But there's something better. You see, these ways require you to long press on some type of key. What happens when you're busy with your hands? Do you have to wash them and dry just to talk to Siri? What if the phone is a little far from reach from you?

All these call for a better and a more iPhone worthy way to summon Siri. And that is the hands-free mode. Yes, all you really have to do to call up Siri is to just say its name. It's just like calling a normal assistant to do stuff you.

But you should know that this is not available by default, you need to activate it yourself in the Settings.

1. Enter the **Settings**
2. Choose the **Siri & search**
3. Turn the switch for **Listen for hey Siri**

Now with this option turned on, things just got a whole lot easier. No more pressing nothing. If you want to call Siri to do something for you, you just say 'Hey Siri'. But when you do this, you want your device to be near you. When it gets too far, Siri will not be able to hear you call its name.

What to say to Siri

Now it's time to get into action. You can get Siri to do a lot of things for you or even to answer a question. But you may find that you keep asking the assistant to do the same things over and over again. Here are a few more things to add variety to your requests.

- 'Hey Siri, call Joshua'
- 'Hey Siri, FaceTime audio call to Mandy
- 'Hey Siri, play me my latest voicemail
- 'Hey Siri, play be the latest voicemail from mike
- 'Hey Siri, call Joe mobile
- 'Hey Siri, call the nearest restaurant
- 'Hey Siri, call Dad on speakerphone
- 'Hey Siri, FaceTime call to Emma
- 'Hey Siri, call 028894
- 'Hey Siri, call mark
- 'Hey Siri, send an email to ken

- 'Hey Siri, Tell Clark I am on my way
- 'Hey Siri, Call the fire department
- 'Hey Siri, Set a timer for 17 minutes
- 'Hey Siri, What's the weather like today
- 'Hey Siri, How many euros are in a pound
- 'Hey Siri, What is 15 percent of 100
- 'Hey Siri, What id 67 divided by 7
- 'Hey Siri, What is the square root of 68
- 'Hey Siri, Take a selfie
- 'Hey Siri, Turn off cellular data
- 'Hey Siri, Turn off Bluetooth
- 'Hey Siri, Open (say the name of the app)
- 'Hey Siri, My mom is Sarah woods. (next time you want to call Sarah, just say call mom)
- 'Hey Siri, Turn down the volume
- 'Hey Siri, Increase the volume to 80%
- 'Hey Siri, What appointments to I have for Monday
- 'Hey Siri, Set an alarm for 9 am
- 'Hey Siri, Turn off all alarms

- 'Hey Siri, What is the synonym for (say word)
- 'Hey Siri, What's the traffic like

Siri jokes

- 'Hey Siri, what is Siri
- 'Hey Siri, what does Siri mean
- 'Hey Siri, are you a robot
- 'Hey Siri, Siri why did Apple make you
- 'Hey Siri, how old are you
- 'Hey Siri, why did the chicken cross the road
- 'Hey Siri, do you smoke
- 'Hey Siri, do you have a boyfriend
- 'Hey Siri, will you marry me
- 'Hey Siri, how do I look
- 'Hey Siri, I am your father
- 'Hey Siri, is john snow dead
- 'Hey Siri, where is Elvis Presley
- 'Hey Siri, sing me a song
- 'Hey Siri, can you rap
- 'Hey Siri, what is the meaning of life
- 'Hey Siri, why
- 'Hey Siri, will pigs fly

Typing to Siri

As mentioned earlier, you can personalize your phone to suit your taste. You can even customize Siri to the way it will be easier for you to use it. if you're the type that doesn't really like talking to a virtual assistant, there's an option for you in the accessibility Settings

It is it's the type to Siri feature. Not everyone likes the idea of talking to Siri and If you would prefer to type to Siri instead, this is how you will go about it.

1. Fire up the **Settings**
2. Then **General**
3. Choose **Accessibility**
4. Select **Siri**
5. Switch on the toggle for **Type To Siri**
6. Now you can type to Siri to get it to do your requests.

Chapter Six

Large Type, Kid Mode and Accessibility

NOTES

The Zoom

If you would like to see the items on the screen of your iPhone device larger, you can consider turning on the option for zoom. And if you find out that the icons on the screen of your device is larger, then you have the zoom option enabled

Here's how to turn it on or off

1. Enter the **Settings**
2. Go to **General**
3. Choose **Accessibility**
4. Select **Zoom**
5. Turn on or off the toggle for **Zoom**

The Magnifier

The magnifier on the iPhone 8 and the 8 Plus is a totally cook option. It does exactly what it says, it magnifies the view. This feature is helpful if you want to a detailed view of something. Maybe you're trying to figure out what's written on the sign, you can just whip out your phone and then use the iPhones camera to get a zoomed view on the information

You can just use the normal zoom of the camera, but when you use the magnifier, you'll be able to get a mega zoom on the area.

1. Launch the **Settings**
2. Choose **General**
3. Tap **Accessibility**
4. Hit **Magnifier**
5. Switch on **Magnifier**

If you want to access the magnifier, you just have to use the home button. Press the home button three times as fast as you can and the magnifier will be open to you. But you should know that if you have other shortcuts like Guided Access enabled, you have to do more than press three times.

To access the magnifier when other things are enabled, press the home button three times and select the option for magnifier. The other shortcuts too will be shown, you can select the others if that's what you want to open.

Call audio routing

Just like other phones, when you make a call or you get a call on your iPhone 8, the audio if the call will come from the earpiece of the phone. You can then be able to change the audio to be played on the speaker. But there's a feature that enables users to be able to get the audio played from another source automatically.

In the settings you will find the call audio routing feature. This feature enables users of the iPhone 8 to be able to select the source in which they want the sound of the calls that they make on the phone to be played.

If this sounds exciting and you would like to access it,
1. Move to the **Settings**
2. Choose **General**
3. Select **Accessibility**

4. Then **Call Audio Routing**

5. Now you want to choose the destination of the call audio

You will be able to select either speaker or a Bluetooth headset. If you choose the Bluetooth headset, the calls will be routed to the headset anytime you answer or make a call. With speaker, you'll be able to get the sound played from the speaker automatically.

Guided access

The guided access is another security feature that you should know about. What this feature basically does is that it locks the phone to just one app. Depending on what you want to use this feature for it can be used for various reasons. But this had proved to be especially helpful for parents.

The reason for this is because parents give the phone to the children when they ask for them to do their homework. They might use it for their homework quite alright, but what happens after. They start to look into where they are not supposed to and find out about your private information.

But with the guided access mode, you sort of guide the use of your phone even while you're not there. The feature will only permit the phone to display that particular app that you set. They will not be able to leave the app or to even access the home screen for that matter.

1. Fire up the **Settings** app
2. Then **General**
3. Tap on **Accessibility**
4. Choose **Guided Access**
5. Switch on **Guided Access**
6. Now you want to tap **Password Settings**
7. Select the **Set Guided Passcode** and enter the passcode
8. You also want to turn on **Accessibility Shortcuts**

If you would like to set the phone to guided access, you just press the home button three times and you have other shortcuts enabled, you will have tap the option for your o enter the guided access mode.

Chapter Seven

Music and Videos

NOTES

How to use the iCloud Music Library

The iCloud Music Library is a very convenient way developed by Apple for users to able to synchronize their music through their different iPhones or iPads. If you would like to make use of the iCloud Music Library, all you have to do is to subscribe to Apple Music. If you're not with Apple Music but you're subscribed to iTunes, you are also good to go

So when you enable this library on your iPhone, you'll have the opportunity of uploading songs from the Apple Music. When you eventually view the library from a different iPhone, you'll see that the songs that you just uploaded would have been added.

If you want to enable the iCloud Music Library

1.   Go to the **Settings**

2. Choose **Music**

3. Select **Library**

4. Turn on the **iCloud Music Library**

You will also be able to choose between the merge and replace option. This provides the different ways that you want your songs to be uploaded. When you choose merge, the old songs will still be available, but when you choose replace, that replaces all the songs.

So now that you've enabled the iCloud Music Library, the question is; how can you then add music to it? Well that's easy. You know that if you want your songs to be available to you on all your devices, you have to make use of the iCloud Music Library.

If you want to add music to it

1. Launch the **Music** app that you want

2. Tap the 3 dot icon that's near the music

3. Choose the **Add To My Music** option

4. The song should be in the **My Music** area

One good thing that that you also want to enable is the option to make a song to be available in offline mode. When you have a song available offline, you don't need to connect to a Wi-Fi network or have cellular data for you access a song. You can just make it available to be listened to offline.

1. Pick the song that you want to save

2. Tap the 3 dot icon

3. Select **Make Available Offline.**

With this option, the song that you just added will available in the Apple Music through your devices. You should find the song or songs if you added plenty in the My Music tab in the library.

As you add songs to the iCloud Music Library from the iPhone 8, you should know that there are some restrictions. While adding music to the library can bring a lot of advantages like you can be able to listen to your music from any device connected to the library, the storage capability is not unlimited. The free storage that the library gives you is just 5GB

Though some of us don't have a large playlist of songs to exceed the 5GB, others do. And if you're the kind that collects music from different genres, artist, albums or the songs of the oldies, the storage space will not be enough. But that's not the end. If you would like more storage, you can just pay to get an extra plan of the iCloud storage.

Also as you include songs to the iTunes iCloud library, you want to make sure that you enabled it. If you don't, you might end up losing your tracks

Apple Music

Apple Music is a music streaming service that was created by Apple. If you've been using, Google Play Music, Spotify, Amazon Music or others, you should be quite familiar with the process. With Apple Music you can have access to some 50 million songs. And these songs can either be downloaded to listen to offline, or be streamed online.

With it, you also get radio stations that are both genre and song based. You are also able to access the Beats 1 radio station. With Apple Music, you can use the iCloud Music Library. All that means is that you are able to get both your Apple Music songs and the songs that you have on your iTunes, gathered in one place for easy access.

There's something that Apple uses to favor its users. They have a wide array of content. You will find that there are some music, albums, music videos or even documentaries which are not available on other services, will be brought to your screen with Apple Music.

If you want to access the content of Apple Music, you need to pay. For you to get the Apple Music at its standard price, it is $9.99 per month. But for students, they don't have to pay the full price, they get a nice discount instead, they pay just $4.99 per month.

If the whole family is interested in using Apple Music, they don't need to pay $9.99 for each member. The family plan is $14.99 per month. And this can cover up to 6 people in the family. You don't need to pay instantly when you start to use Apple Music. Users get a free trial of 3 months.

Adding from Apple Music to library

You can transfer music, video, playlist and albums from the Apple Music to your own music library as long as you are subscribed to Apple Music. And if you would like to see the content on your Apple Music library on all you devices, you just have to turn on the iCloud music library and add the song to it. You should be able to access it as long as you use the same Apple ID

If you would like to add a song from the Apple Music to your own personal library,

1. Open up the **Music** app
2. Move to the songs that you would like to add
3. Hit the Plus button beside the title
4. If you are viewing the song in the full screen playback control, you can still access the button at the bottom left corner

If you might not want to add a single song, you might be interested in adding an entire album, playlist for the Apple Music to your own music library. All you have to do

1. Launch the **Music** app
2. Move to the album or playlist that you want to include
3. Hit the button that says **+ADD**.

You should know that after you've made the content available in your library, you must still have internet connection for you to able to listen to it.

Creating playlist

These days everyone has a playlist. When you create a playlist to compile your songs, it's very easy for you to reach a particular group of songs. And just like other services, iTunes enables users to be able to create custom playlist to add their favorite songs in.

Since creating iTunes playlist is so easy that everyone knows how to do it, the trend now is to create a playlist on your iTunes and then connect it to your phone. But you don't always have to do that. You can still create them from your iPhone. If you have playlist created on your device, you'll be able to reach a collection of songs easily.

You just tell Siri to play a particular playlist rather than say play this, play that and then this. If you want to create a playlist,

1. Move to the **Music** app

2. Select playlist in the **Library** segment
3. Select the **New Playlist**
4. Now you can add a name for the playlist you want to create
5. What is a playlist if you don't have music in it to listen to? Hit the **Add Music** option and choose the songs to add

As you listen to that particular playlist, you will want to add some other songs to it. You don't need to create a new playlist and then adding the new songs to it

1. Open the **Music** app
2. Choose **Playlist**
3. Tap the playlist that you want to update
4. At the upper corner, choose the **Edit**
5. Select **Add Music**
6. Select the songs that you want to add. You can locate it manually or you can use the search option to find the song
7. Touch the + to add the music.

The iTunes store

With the iTunes store on our iPhone, you should have no problem with media shopping. The iTunes will give you the opportunity to purchase a particular song or a full album. With all the collection in apple's catalog, you can choose to either buy or rent content

While you will surely be enticed to get the latest movie, that's not all you're restricted to. You also able to access old movies and view the previous seasons and episodes of your favorite TV show. So if you're the type that loves your iPhone packed with the hottest media both music or video, the iTunes store is for you.

Getting movies from the iTunes is no rocket science. All you just have to do first before you start to think of downloading anything is making sure that you have an Apple ID. This is what you will use with iTunes. You make sure of that and you have no problem

1. Fire up the **iTunes store**
2. Locate the media you want to download. There different ways for you to look for the movie, music or TV show that you want to download
   - Go through the different categories for the music, movies TV shows
   - Or better still, since you know the particular media you want to download, you can just hit the **Search button** and you can search for it either by the title, the genre, the artist or others
3. When you find the media that you want to buy, tap it
4. Hit the button to buy that is at the top corner of the display. That is for if you want to buy the whole album or season. It will show the price. But if you're

interested in getting just one particular media, hit the buy at next to the song or episode. This too will show the price

5. Hit the **Buy Button** another time
6. Input the Apple ID password
7. Hit **Ok.**

TV app

The TV app that you get on the iPad and on the iPhone 8 takes the place of the Video app. This TV app was available in the United States but it is also available in UK. What this TV app does essentially is that it combines the TV shows, movies from all the services or apps that you use in one place.

The TV app was created to be like the main headquarters for all your TV shows and movies. Not only does it show your movies, it can also tap into your iTunes library, your apps and the different services that you are subscribed to.

In previous versions of the iOS, you would not find the TV app. What was available back then was the Video app. But on the iPhone 8, what you have is the new TV app for you to find out new content to view on your iPhone.

Now you must be hyped up to find out how you can get the TV app on your iPhone. Well you see, you don't you really don't have to go looking the app store for the app. All you just have to do is to make sure that that you have the latest iOS on your device

So if you don't have the latest iOS version, you want to make sure that you update it. After you update, you should see the TV on your home screen. If you don't find it there, you can just use the search option in your phone to find it. Trust me it has got to be there. You don't need to do anything, the TV app will just appear instead of the video app.

Chapter Eight

The Camera

NOTES

Camera app quick launch

When it comes to taking photos on your iPhone, what you want make sure is that you do it fast. Those times when you are on vacation or you're chilling at the beach, you get to experience different sights and sounds. As you see these things, the first thing that comes to your mind is to preserve the memory

And what better way to preserve a moment in time than with pictures. So you whip out your phone quickly, and then you try to navigate to the camera app but you're having a hard time finding it. In no time, the moment that you're trying to capture is gone, but that's not the only time this would happen. Every time, you find that you keep missing the moments you want to capture

But that has to end. There are many ways for you to fire up the camera app quickly. With these methods, the camera app is opened in no time and you would be able to take your shot,

Method 1

One of the best ways that will guarantee you a fast and easy opening of the camera app is through the lock screen. If you would like to go through with the method,

1. Press the power button to switch to the lock screen of your device

2. When the screen comes on, the display that will be shown will be the lock screen. From the lock screen, swipe left. Just like that my friend, the camera app is opened to you

Just so easy, if you've got a long passcode, you don't have to start fiddling with the numbers to enter the code. This is even one of the reasons why you miss the moment that you want to capture. All you have to is swipe left from the screen

Method 2

The next easy way to launch the camera app is through the control center. The previous method that we talked about will come in handy when the screen is locked. But when you're using the phone to either play a game or surf an app, you don't have to press the power button to lock the phone and the swipe to enter the camera. All you have to do to fire the camera app up is through the control center

1. For you to get to the control center on your iPhone, you just slide up from the lower part of the screen

2. When you look at the bottom corner of the screen, you'll find the camera app. Just tap it to launch it.

This method is very beneficial when you are making use of your phone and you want to take a picture.

Method 3

The last method we are going to be talking about is getting it through he home screen. But this is not the normal app list on the home screen. We are going to fix the camera app at the area that we will be able to access it quickly. You can just get the app directly from the app screen. But when you go through it from that area, it's no different from the normal way.

But do you see the group of apps that is located at the bottom part of the screen, this area of where the apps are is called the dock. When you have the camera app in dock, you can just tap the camera icon when you are in the home screen, you don't have to start swiping to the control center or going to the lock screen.

But the issue now is how we are going to add the camera icon to the dock. This is no hard task. You just need to press and hold on the app while you're in the home screen of the iPhone 8. When you press and hold, don't release your grip until you see the app shake. When the app shakes that's the sign for you to drag it to the dock. Now when you've moved the app to the dock, you can release.

So far, we talked about three ways you can launch the camera app in a second. These three ways are really useful in the three situations that you might have your phone in. You might have your phone in your pocket, bag or purse. And when you have your phone like that, you don't need to get out of the lock screen and unlock your phone. Just do it right from the lock screen and slide left.

The other situation that you might have your phone in is in usage mode. No matter what you use your phone to do, you will be able to access the camera app. If the screen that you are makes to get into the control center, then the camera app is just a tap away

Or the phone might be in the home screen. Even then, you don't need to start looking for the camera the old fashioned way. When you side load the camera app to the dock, you'll be able to find the camera app easily when you're in the home screen.

Taking your camera skills to the next level with HDR

You might have been seeing some down to the earth photos that those pro photographers take. The photos get the right exposure and everything just seems to be equally balanced. When it comes to the right exposure with your iPhone, you don't need to go to photography school to be able to know how to shoot it right.

They know the secret to taking the photos at the right exposure and color and its time you learn it too. It is the HDR. Now what is that? You see, the HDR is short for High Dynamic Range. When you're in a scene that has got high contrast, the normal camera mode can find it hard to get the details.

You might find that it will easily capture the details in the shadows but the whites will be too bright without details or vice versa. But when you use HDR, you will have your photos well lit and the colors in the image will become vivid.

If you would like to make use of the HDR mode

1. Launch the **Settings**
2. Then choose **Camera**
3. You want to make sure that the **Smart HDR** or **Auto HDR** mode is turned off. If it is on you will not be able to select it in the camera screen
4. Now open the **Camera** app
5. From the top of the screen, hit the icon for **HDR**

Photo mode

With the iPhone 8 and the iPhone 8 Plus, you have different modes to take photos in. if you want to access the modes, you just have to slide the screen. With each mode, you have different effects to your photos. The first mode you get on the carousel is the Photo mode.

The Photo mode in the iPhone 8 camera is just the standard camera mode. Unlike the others, what you get with the Photo mode is just the exactly what the camera gives you with no unnecessary effects or filters. But with this Photo mode, you are still able to make use of the live photos option. This live photo makes your pictures animated and you'll see the images move. More on that soon though.

With this Photo mode, you will have your photos looking right. This is because the camera will have the object you are taking a shot of to be focused and the exposure too will be set in a way that the image doesn't get dim. The focusing of the image will be so that the background and the subject that you are shooting will be displayed perfectly.

But still you can adjust the exposure at which the images are taken. If you want the image to be taken at the exposure that you want it to be, you just have to tap the screen. The moment before you take the shot, tap the place that you want to the exposure to be changed.

You can also long press on the screen for you to be able to set the focus and the exposure

Live photos

Now let's talk about live photos on your iPhone. We just talked about how taking photos is the best way to preserve memories and moments. Well the live photos option is even better. The live photos feature does just as it says; it makes your photos come alive.

When you take a normal picture, it's always a frozen image. But with live photos, the image does not have to be frozen, you'll get the moment and the action of what is going on in the photo for 3 seconds.

When you take a picture with the live photos option, the camera records 1.5 seconds before you tap the shutter and 1.5 after. Giving you a 3 second photo capturing both sound and movement.

If you want to make use of the live photos option,

1. Go to the **Camera** app
2. Select live photos from the options

You can give your photos a lot of effects with live photos, you can choose between Live, Loop, Long Exposure or Bounce

Portrait mode

You might be aware of the rave of using portrait mode for your photo. Well portrait mode does deserve the attention it's getting. What is portrait mode anyway? Basically the portrait mode is one of the shooting modes that you have on the iPhone 8 plus.

You see that that photo that your friend said she took with her iPhone camera but you did not believe and thought it was a DSLR? Well she is right. It is with her iPhone camera but in portrait mode. When the camera is set to portrait mode, it will automatically blur the background of the subject you're trying to shoot.

But this does not mean that the subject themselves will be blurred. They'll be sharp and clear as possible. So when a photo is taken with a blurry background but crisp subject, you tend to take it as a professional photo. Add a bit of editing to the mix and you could have sworn it was with a professional camera.

Most times, the background of the photo can be busy. While you can just take a photo with the normal camera mode, the image will become distracting that way. But when you make use of the portrait mode, the noise in the background is reduced and the subject stands out clear

If you want to use the portrait mode for your photos

1. Fire up the **Camera** app
2. The camera might be in the normal photo mode. Swipe on the screen to access the portrait mode.

While using the portrait mode can be thrilling, you want to know some few things before you start.

First, low light is a No when it comes to portrait mode. The shooting mode will not work well in low light. In fact it will even notify with a message saying that it needs more light to shoot.

Second, you also want to make sure of the distance of your subject to the camera. You want the subject to be around 2 to 8 feet from the phones camera.

Square mode

Another mode that you have on the iPhone 8 camera is the square mode. The name is fitting because it restricts the image to a square. When you set the camera to this mode, the image will be fitted to a square. This mode is not usually used and you may not use it much.

But when you're trying to upload something like profile picture online, you might want to consider this mode. For profile pictures, it is recommended that your photos are not oblong or too wide. And when you take a selfie or a normal picture, you notice that you don't always have your shots squared.

So when you try to upload, you have to edit it and crop out important sections in the image. But with the square mode, you don't need to start doing an after editing to crop out the image.

When you set the camera to square mode, the image is shot in square already and all you have to do is upload it directly.

With this option you don't have important detail cropped out. If there's something that you want to appear in the photo, all you just have to do is set the camera to show it.

Disclaimer

In as much as the author believes beginners will find this book helpful in learning how to use the iPhone 8/8 plus, it is only a small book. It should not be relied upon solely for all iPhone tricks and troubleshooting.

About the author

Stephen Rock has been a certified apps developer and tech researcher for more than 12 years. Some of his 'how to' guides have appeared in a handful of international journals and tech blogs. He loves rabbits. 9